AF746574

JOBS IN DESIGN & CONSTRUCTION

PETER TURNER

WORKING IN AUSTRALIA

REDBACK publishing

First published 2023 by
Redback Publishing
Australia

www.redbackpublishing.com.au
orders@redbackpublishing.com.au

ISBN 978-1-761400-34-6 PBK

Author: Peter Turner
Editor: Caroline Thomas
Designer: Redback Publishing

Originated by Redback Publishing

A catalogue record for this book is available from the National Library of Australia

Acknowledgements
Abbreviations: l—left, r—right, b—bottom, t—top, c—centre, m—middle
We would like to thank the following for permission to reproduce photographs: (Images © shutterstock)

p27 Phil Pettitt / Courtesy of Phil and Carla Pettitt
28 Cristian Zamfir / Shutterstock

CONTENTS

DESIGN AND CONSTRUCTION

All the things you use every day – the bed you sleep in, the house you live in, the scooter you ride on, your digital devices and the packages that things come in – have all been designed by a team of people and then constructed by different teams of people.

DESIGN

KEY WORK AREAS

- Design disciplines are often grouped into three broad areas: physical, industrial and visual communication
- Physical designers include architects, interior designers, landscape designers, and television, film and theatre set designers
- Visual communicators include commercial artists, exhibition designers and display designers
- Other design roles include textile, fashion and furniture designers

JOBS IN DESIGN

The term, designer, refers to a broad grouping of people. Designers are concerned with a product's aesthetics, which are how it looks, its function and the technical requirements needed to make it. Jobs in design require a combination of creative flair and technical knowledge.

DESIGN AND ENGINEERING

Many engineering roles focus on design. A central part of an engineer's role can involve looking at how a product or system could be improved through small changes. Engineers need to be highly creative and lateral thinkers, but not necessarily artistic, which is a trait that is required to work as a designer.

CONSTRUCTION

KEY WORK AREAS

- ***Skilled construction workers***
  People who operate earthmoving equipment and machines. They include backhoe operators, pipe layers, concrete workers, scaffolders, crane operators, riggers and doggers.
- ***Skilled tradespeople***
  People who have completed an apprenticeship, which can take up to four years. They include, electricians, carpenters, plumbers and gasfitters, boilermakers, and fitter and turners.
- ***Building technicians***
  People who work on and off site including drafters, building inspectors, administrators and site supervisors. TAFEs offer a range of certificate, diploma and advanced diplomas and some people study at university for a bachelor's degree in building construction, construction science or construction management.
- ***Managers and professionals***
  People who have completed university degrees and continually update their skills through professional development and further study. This category includes project managers, architects, civil and structural engineers, professional builders, building surveyors and land surveyors.

THE IMPORTANCE OF MATHS

Most jobs in design and construction require a good understanding of maths. People who work in the design and construction industries use mathematical knowledge when taking measurements, working out angles, calculating the quantity of materials required for a particular job, and determining surface area. In most jobs related to design and construction, people use maths every day.

BUILDING AND CONSTRUCTION MATERIALS

There are a range of job opportunities in the production of materials for the building, construction and manufacturing industries. These materials include steel, timber, bricks, glass, plastics, concrete, ceramics, rubber and granite. Work places include mines, quarries, steelworks, foundries, engineering workshops, smelters, plantation forests, sawmills, recycling plants and laboratories.

TIMBER/ FOREST WORKER

JOB DESCRIPTION

Timber and forest workers usually work in plantation forests, sawmills or timber yards.

RANGE OF WORK:

- operate saws to convert logs to usable timber
- stack, load and transport timber using forklifts
- produce timber finishes such as veneers and laminates
- assemble pre-fabricated products such as window frames
- fill timber orders and keep records

EDUCATION AND TRAINING

Timber and forest workers are often trained on-the-job. Certificate qualifications and Advanced Diplomas can enhance employment opportunities.

CONCRETE AND STONE MACHINE OPERATOR

JOB DESCRIPTION

Concrete and stone machine operators use machines to make bricks, tiles, pipes, railway sleepers and structural beams.

RANGE OF WORK:

- control settings on machines
- position material on machines
- adjust valves to feed and control the flow of substances such as sand and cement
- check products for quality and clean the machines

EDUCATION AND TRAINING

Training is usually done on-the-job. There are several courses at certificate level.

SHEET METAL WORKER (LIGHT FABRICATION)

JOB DESCRIPTION

Sheet metal workers use a range of hand tools and equipment, including Computer Numerically Controlled (CNC) machines, to make products and components using thin sheet metal. These materials can include galvanised steel, stainless steel, aluminium, copper and brass.

RANGE OF WORK:

- read detailed drawings and specifications
- mark out and cut sheet metal
- join parts by riveting, bolting, welding or soldering
- finish products by cleaning, polishing, filing or bathing them

EDUCATION AND TRAINING

People can become sheet metal workers by undertaking an apprenticeship that combines on-the-job training with TAFE qualifications.

MY STORY

After finishing school, I wanted to work with my hands in construction. I did a Diploma in Construction Material Testing and got a job at a quarry in the quality control department, making sure all of the products fit the specifications before they are dispatched.

I start work at 6am and start with a visual check of the piles to make sure they look okay. Then we go out and collect samples from different parts of the quarry, using loaders, shovels or chute samplers. After collecting the samples we do lots of tests. We use sieves and magnifying glasses to look at the rocks and then we test the strength of the stones. To test the cement we add chemicals to it and then monitor any changes such as its temperature. We then enter the data from the tests into the computer, which indicates if the samples meet the required specifications.

A few words of advice:
It's a good industry for people who like manual work and being outside, and there are plenty of opportunities.

ADAM BUTTERWORTH
MATERIALS TESTER

'It's a good industry for people who like manual work'

DESIGNING BUILDINGS

The first stage of a building project is the design phase. People usually think of architects when they think of building design, but many people play important roles during this stage. Architects call on a range of technical experts to advise them on various things, such as the quality of the soil in an area and the foundations required to support a building.

ENGINEERS

JOB DESCRIPTION

Depending on the size of a building and the site, there can be three or more engineers involved at the design stage. Their role is to ensure the building can withstand all weather conditions and stand up to the pressure of heavy traffic, vibration and other elements.

EDUCATION AND TRAINING

All engineers complete an engineering degree at university. Many engineers undertake further study to specialise in an area. Engineers possess high-level technical knowledge. They must also be good at solving problems and communicating their technical advice to a range of people.

RANGE OF ENGINEERS:

- ***Geotechnical engineer*** – Geotechnical engineers understand how the soil and rock beneath a proposed building site will react under pressure. They collect and analyse soil samples and rocks, prepare reports and advise on the foundations required to support the building.
- ***Structural engineer*** – Structural engineers understand the stress and pressure that wind, waves, earthquakes, cyclones and floods, people and vehicles can place on a building. They specify the type, quantities and placement of materials and reinforcing that will strengthen a building to withstand these stresses.
- ***Building services engineer*** – Building services engineers are involved with designing the amenities needed in large buildings. They advise on the heating, air-conditioning, lighting, power, water and gas supplies, plumbing, drainage and fire safety exits. These amenities ensure a building is both functional and safe.

ARCHITECTURAL DRAFTER

JOB DESCRIPTION

Architectural drafters carry out technical support functions using Computer Aided Design (CAD) software. They are employed by architect firms or by building design companies.

RANGE OF WORK:

- measure sites
- develop and refine designs
- prepare drawings with detailed elevations, sections, building materials, plumbing and drainage
- examine building codes and laws

EDUCATION AND TRAINING

Completion of a TAFE certificate, diploma or advanced diploma is required to become a registered architectural drafter or building designer.

ARCHITECT

JOB DESCRIPTION

Architects draw on their creative abilities and technical knowledge to design buildings that are safe, appealing, within a set budget and compliant with regulations. Most architects work for private architectural firms.

RANGE OF WORK:

- talk to clients about their needs, ideas and budget
- write submissions and tenders
- prepare hand-sketched concept drawings and production drawings
- prepare digital drawings using Computer Aided Design (CAD) software
- make models
- arrange building and planning permits
- choose and prepare specifications for building materials, surfaces, fittings and finishes
- monitor building construction and negotiate with builders.

EDUCATION AND TRAINING

A five-year degree specialising in architecture is essential to become a registered architect.

MY STORY

'studying art or graphics is a great preparation for architecture'

When I first graduated, I mainly worked on corporate projects. Corporate work is good because budgets are usually big, but there is less involvement with the users of the building and it tends to be driven by formulas. The firm I work for now does a lot of community work, such as visitor information centres, schools, libraries, lifesaving clubs and community centres, which is more fulfilling.

I'm involved in a primary school library, which is in the construction phase, so I have fortnightly meetings with the builder and the client. Architects need skills in many areas – creativity, design and aesthetic skills are essential and maths is very important.

A few words of advice:
As well as subjects such as maths and physics, studying art or graphics is a great preparation for architecture.

MEGAN HARRISON
ARCHITECT

BUILDING HOUSES

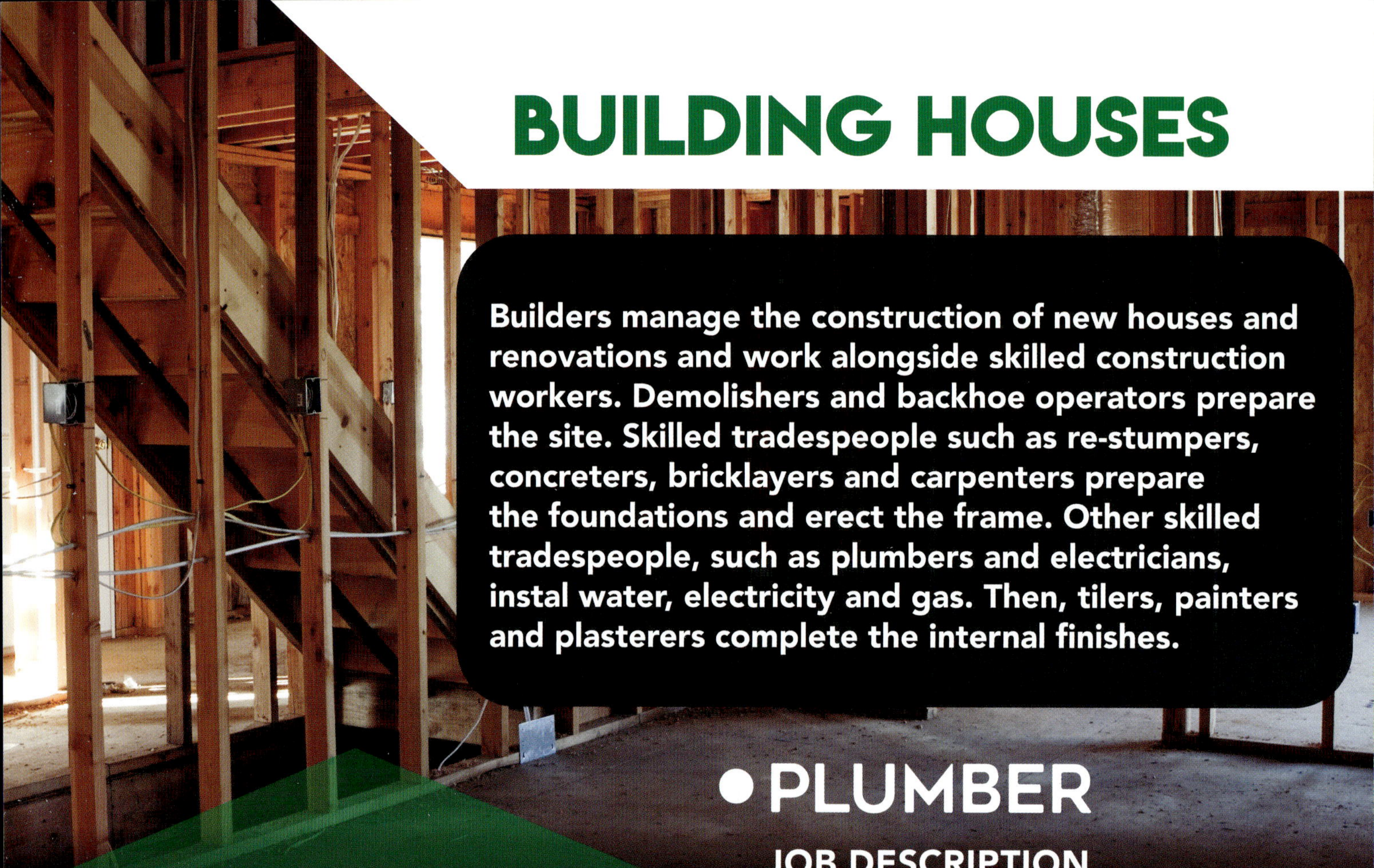

Builders manage the construction of new houses and renovations and work alongside skilled construction workers. Demolishers and backhoe operators prepare the site. Skilled tradespeople such as re-stumpers, concreters, bricklayers and carpenters prepare the foundations and erect the frame. Other skilled tradespeople, such as plumbers and electricians, instal water, electricity and gas. Then, tilers, painters and plasterers complete the internal finishes.

• BUILDER

JOB DESCRIPTION

Builders oversee the construction process from the time the contract is signed with a client until the time the building is completed. Builders require good technical skills and good financial management skills.

RANGE OF WORK:

- prepare quotes and building contracts
- coordinate contractors and tradespeople on site
- choose, source and order materials
- liaise with architects, clients and engineers
- supervise workers on site to ensure work quality
- solve technical problems
- keep project costs on budget and on time

EDUCATION AND TRAINING

In Australia, each state has different requirements. Generally, to become a builder, a person completes a degree, diploma or associate diploma from a university or TAFE, then goes on to complete a number of years of hands-on experience.

• PLUMBER

JOB DESCRIPTION

Plumbers lay and repair pipes and drains, and instal and connect pipes and water to the wet areas in houses.

RANGE OF WORK:

- read plans and technical drawings
- mark positions for connections
- insert pipes through walls and floors
- instal toilets, showers and sinks
- maintain and repair plumbing systems

AREAS OF SPECIALISATION

- *Drainers* instal and repair stormwater and sanitation systems.
- *Roofing plumbers* instal and repairs roofs, gutters and downpipes.
- *Irrigation instalers* focus on watering systems for large areas, such as golf courses.

EDUCATION AND TRAINING

Plumbers need to complete an apprenticeship in plumbing and gasfitting, which can take up to four years and combines study with on-the-job learning. Additional training and licences are required to work in specialist areas.

• CARPENTER

JOB DESCRIPTION

After the foundations have been laid, it is the role of the carpenter to erect the timber and/or steel frames. Carpenters also lay timber floors, pitch roofs and instal windows and doors.

EDUCATION AND TRAINING

To become a qualified carpenter people study for a certificate in carpentry. Also, you need to complete an apprenticeship in carpentry and joinery. Pre-apprenticeships in carpentry and joinery are also available.

• STONEMASON

JOB DESCRIPTION

Builders contract stonemasons to cut and shape hard and soft slabs of rock and blocks into kitchen benchtops and bathroom vanity tops. Stonemasons also lay stone, granite and marble floor tiles and outdoor paving.

EDUCATION AND TRAINING

An apprenticeship in stonemasonry leads to entry to this specialised trade.

MY STORY

I always liked woodwork at school and I left school when I found a job as a factoryhand at a kitchen manufacturer. I thought it might lead to a cabinetmaking apprenticeship, which it did. I worked for two employers before starting my own cabinetmaking business. I specialise in kitchens.

My work involves sitting down with people to plan a kitchen, and finding out what they like and what they want. We put the design onto a computer so they can see what it is going to look like, and if they like it, I go out and take all the measurements.

To make a good cabinet you have to be very fussy. It's critical that you are precise at every step of the process. You need to be good at maths because you take a lot of measurements and you have to make sure you double-check everything you do.

Cabinet making is a good trade. You get to build something different every day and the materials you use are always changing.

A few words of advice:
Do an apprenticeship if you want to become a cabinetmaker. It's great to get a trade behind you. Then if you do want to try something else, you can do it because you'll always have this qualification.

'It's great to get a trade behind you.'

TONY GALEA
CABINETMAKER

COMMERCIAL CONSTRUCTION

The construction of large-scale buildings, such as shopping centres, office towers, hotels, hospitals and universities, can involve hundreds of people with a diverse range of skills.

• EXCAVATOR OPERATOR

JOB DESCRIPTION

Excavator operators help to prepare and level building sites before construction begins. They operate heavy earthmoving machinery such as backhoes, bulldozers, graders and scrapers to excavate, push and remove soil, rocks, trees and rubble. Excavator operators work in hot, wet, dusty and noisy conditions, although often their machinery has soundproofing and airconditioning.

RANGE OF WORK:

- transfer soil and rock from the ground to dumping trucks
- follow drawings under the direction of supervisors and engineers
- clean, lubricate and refuel equipment

EDUCATION AND TRAINING

Excavator operators have usually worked as labourers before training on-the-job as excavator operators.

• CRANE OPERATOR AND DOGGER

JOB DESCRIPTION

Cranes are used to lift, move and place heavy objects on construction sites. On building sites, the role of a crane operator is usually to check that cranes are level before lifting and moving the cranes into position.

RANGE OF WORK:

- apply slings to loads lifted by cranes
- direct the cranes' movements
- check the size and weight of the loads to be moved
- signal to the crane operators using hand signals, two-way radios and whistle signals

EDUCATION AND TRAINING

To work as a crane operator you must receive a High Risk Work license for the class of crane you want to operate.

BUILDING SURVEYOR

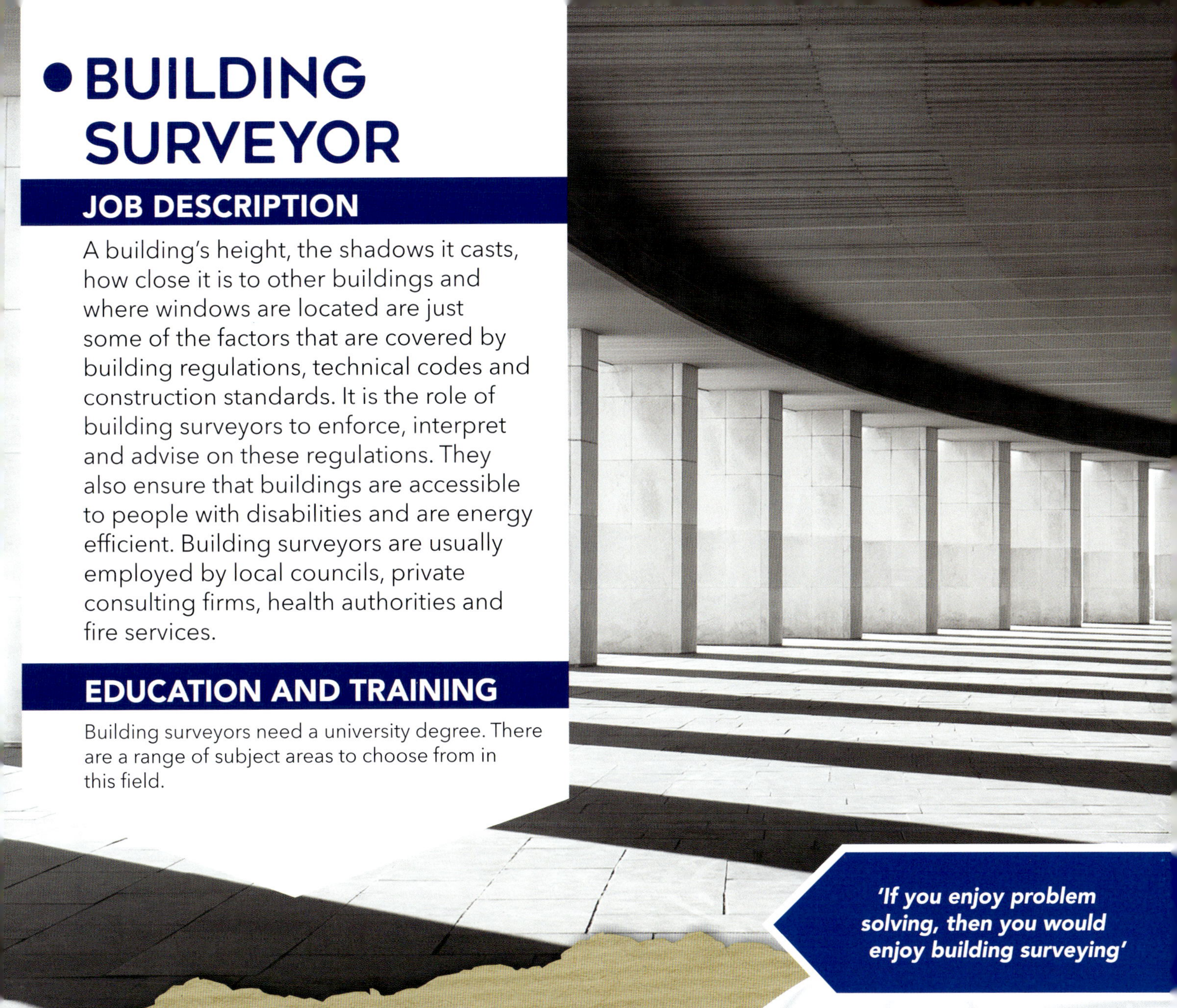

JOB DESCRIPTION

A building's height, the shadows it casts, how close it is to other buildings and where windows are located are just some of the factors that are covered by building regulations, technical codes and construction standards. It is the role of building surveyors to enforce, interpret and advise on these regulations. They also ensure that buildings are accessible to people with disabilities and are energy efficient. Building surveyors are usually employed by local councils, private consulting firms, health authorities and fire services.

EDUCATION AND TRAINING

Building surveyors need a university degree. There are a range of subject areas to choose from in this field.

'If you enjoy problem solving, then you would enjoy building surveying'

MY STORY

I work in building surveying and moved into access consulting three years ago. My main role is to look at drawings and, as part of a design team, provide advice to architects, owners and builders about how they can make their buildings more accessible to people with disabilities. We advise and write reports on ways to make the signage clear and legible, and on hearing systems for theatres and conference rooms. I then carry out site inspections to make sure our advice is implemented.

A few words of advice:
If you have an analytical mind, pay close attention to detail and enjoy problem solving, then you would enjoy building surveying.

KAREN CHUNG
BUILDING SURVEYOR

CIVIL CONSTRUCTION

The civil construction sector includes people involved in the designing, building, maintaining and repairing of roads, bridges, tunnels, railways, sewerage systems, power plants and harbours. Civil construction work can range from the resurfacing of a road, to the completion of a new freeway or railway line. As well as design and construction work, many people in civil construction are involved in testing, research, development and consulting roles.

• SHOTFIRER

JOB DESCRIPTION

Often, soil and rocks have to be removed, trenches made or buildings demolished before work on a road, bridge, tunnel or other infrastructure projects can begin. It is the role of the construction shotfirer (also known as a blaster) to conduct blasting operations using explosives.

RANGE OF WORK:

- inspect the site before and after the blast
- assess the type and quantities of explosives needed
- ensure the safety of workers on site
- insert detonators and charges into holes

EDUCATION AND TRAINING

To work as a shotfirer, a shotfirer licence is required. Regulations about the licence can differ from state to state.

• EARTHMOVER

JOB DESCRIPTION

There are a range of heavy earthmoving vehicles used in civil construction, including bulldozers, excavators, front end loaders, graders, scrapers and skid-steer loaders. Earthmovers work outdoors, often in hot, dusty, muddy and noisy conditions.

RANGE OF WORK:

- select and operate attachments for the machinery
- interpret and follow markers using heavy machinery
- break up rock and excavate earth to the correct levels and alignment
- maintain earthmoving equipment

EDUCATION AND TRAINING

Earthmovers must be 18 years of age or older. They have usually worked as labourers on a construction site before moving into this type of role. Training is usually available on-the-job.

CIVIL ENGINEER

JOB DESCRIPTION

Civil engineers are responsible for producing safe, structurally sound and economically viable structures.

RANGE OF WORK:

- investigate sites to work out the most suitable foundation for a proposed construction
- research and advise on the best engineering solution to meet a client's needs and budget
- produce detailed designs and documentation for the construction and implementation of civil engineering projects
- organise the delivery of materials needed for the construction project
- develop detailed programs for the coordination of site activities

SPECIALISATION

Civil engineers are usually employed by construction companies, engineering consulting firms, government departments, local councils, university research facilities or utility operators.

RANGE OF SPECIALISATIONS:

- project management
- highway engineering
- railway engineering
- structural engineering

EDUCATION AND TRAINING

Civil engineers must have an engineering degree, which usually takes four years. This enables graduates to become a member of Engineers Australia, the peak professional organisation for engineers in Australia. It is common for civil engineers to then seek further training or qualifications in an area of specialty.

'continue with maths and science at school'

MY STORY

I did a bachelor of civil engineering combined with a bachelor of science because I wanted to help create a better environment through the infrastructure we use every day; the roads, bridges and buildings we live and work in.

I'm in the infrastructure team at an engineering consulting firm and mainly work on the structural design of bridges.

The architect sets out what they want the bridge to look like, how wide, how deep, the colour and shape, and then the structural engineers figure out the materials required. We'll then do a basic hand sketch with written instructions and a draftsperson will add greater detail.

As an engineer you never stop learning. It is a very rewarding career because the products you are designing will have a real influence on people, whether it's a bridge, a water treatment plant or an energy-saving car.

A few words of advice:
When you are at school it is so important to keep your options open. This is best achieved by continuing with maths and science, even though it can be hard work. These are the subjects that will give you options.

REBECCA BARKER
STRUCTURAL ENGINEER

ENERGY: DESIGN AND CONSTRUCTION

Electricity provides power to everything from lights, to heavy machinery. There are many sources of electricity. The most common sources of electricity are fossil fuels, particularly coal. However, a growing number of people are researching, designing and building systems and structures that use alternative sources of electricity including the sun and wind.

ELECTRICAL ENGINEER

JOB DESCRIPTION

Electrical engineers design and build systems and machines that generate, transmit, control and use electrical energy. They can specialise in an area such as electrical maintenance, electrical power, telecommunications, computers, generators, motors and transformers.

RANGE OF WORK:

- plan and design power stations
- design and produce drawings of electrical systems using Computer Aided Design (CAD)
- make or improve electrical products such as engines or components for appliances
- design and instal signalling devices to control road, rail and air traffic

EDUCATION AND TRAINING

To become an electrical engineer you need to complete a four-year degree in electrical engineering.

• ELECTRICAL LINESPERSON

JOB DESCRIPTION

An electrical linesperson constructs, repairs and maintains overhead lines and cables carrying electricity to homes, commercial and industrial users, and train services. Electrical linespeople also work on street lighting and metering systems, which record power usage.

RANGE OF WORK:

- inspect poles and towers
- instal power poles, wires, circuit breakers and switches
- perform emergency repairs
- cover wires with insulated materials
- trim tree branches and keep power lines clear

EDUCATION AND TRAINING

Electrical linespersons need an apprenticeship, which usually takes four years and combines on-the-job training with study. To be a linesperson you must enjoy working outdoors, be able to work at heights and be good with manual work.

• CABLE JOINTER

JOB DESCRIPTION

Electricity cables are used in the transmission and distribution of electricity to homes, offices and factories. It is the role of the cable jointer to make and repair joins in the power supply and control cables.

RANGE OF WORK:

- read and update diagrams for the layout of cable systems
- instal and replace cables
- pull electrical cables through underground pipes
- prepare low and high voltage cable joints
- be involved in the manufacturing of cable jointing components
- encase cables in protective covers

EDUCATION AND TRAINING

Cable jointers need to complete an apprenticeship or traineeship.

'Physics is the most useful subject to study'

MY STORY

I did an honours degree in physics and then a PhD in the field of solar power applications. I now jointly own and manage a small company that designs and instals solar energy systems. People often come to us because they need to provide power to a piece of equipment or a house that is some distance from a normal power source. In remote country areas we design systems that use solar energy to power everything in the building- the lights, TV and all the appliances. It can take a lot of design work to come up with the best solution to meet the needs of clients.

When I joined the industry in 1987, there were about 100 people in Australia working in the industry. Now it is a booming industry. It's nice to have chosen a career where I get up in the morning, go to work, come home and think the world's a better place for me having done my work.

A few words of advice:
Physics is the most useful subject to study so that you understand electricity, solar energy and batteries. But a PhD in physics is certainly not necessary to work in the area. You could look at doing electrical or mechanical engineering, an electrical trades course, or a TAFE certificate course in renewable energy.

RICHARD POTTER
MANAGING DIRECTOR
SOLAR COMPANY

RAIL AND AEROSPACE

Australia's rail industry employs over 100,000 people. There are three main areas in the Australian aerospace industry: design and manufacturing, research and development and airworthiness operations.

AEROSPACE ENGINEER

JOB DESCRIPTION

Aerospace engineers are employed by airline operators, the Civil Aviation Authority, manufacturers of aeroplanes and aircraft components, the Royal Australian Air Force (RAAF) and defence organisations. Their role is to design, develop, manufacture and maintain flight vehicles, such as aeroplanes, helicopters, missiles, gliders and spacecraft.

RANGE OF WORK:

- design aircraft , aircraft components and support equipment, often using Computer Aided Design (CAD) software
- conduct tests to measure the performance or airworthiness of aircraft
- design and oversee maintenance schedules
- investigate and resolve problems with autopilot, instrument and navigation systems
- inspect and resolve mechanical problems with the mechanical components including the landing gear, wheels and brakes systems
- evaluate new and used aircraft
- participate in flight tests

EDUCATION AND TRAINING

To become an aerospace engineer, you would complete an engineering degree at university with a major in aeronautical or aerospace engineering.

RAILWAY ENGINEER

JOB DESCRIPTION

Railway engineers are usually civil engineers who have gained extensive experience in the railways industry or have undertaken further qualifications. It is an industry that uses highly sophisticated technology. Railway engineers usually specialise in areas such as the design, construction and maintenance of bridges, tunnels, train tracks and train signalling. A railway engineer's focus is on making trains safer, faster, smoother, more reliable and on reducing wear and corrosion of the track.

EDUCATION AND TRAINING

Railway engineers have usually undertaken a bachelor of civil engineering. They might also complete postgraduate qualifications specialising in rail.

RAILWAY TRACK WORKER

JOB DESCRIPTION

A railway track worker lays, repairs, and cleans tracks. This may involve positioning and fastening rails, cutting and grinding rails, bolting and welding rail sections, and keeping the track clear of vegetation. The work can be physically demanding and involve working in hot, dusty or wet conditions for long periods. Railway track workers commonly work shiftwork.

EDUCATION AND TRAINING

Although there are no minimum qualifications to work as a railway track worker, qualifications are available to prepare and train people in this role. There is also as-on-the-job training available.

AIRCONDITIONING AND REFRIGERATION MECHANIC

JOB DESCRIPTION

Airconditioning and refrigeration systems are critical for passenger and driver comfort, particularly for those driving freight trains and for the transportation of perishable food. It is the role of the airconditioning and refrigeration mechanic to assemble, instal, service and test these cooling systems. Airconditioning and refrigeration mechanics often work with electricians and carpenters during the instalation of these systems.

EDUCATION AND TRAINING

Education involves apprenticeships and the completion of a certificate level qualification.

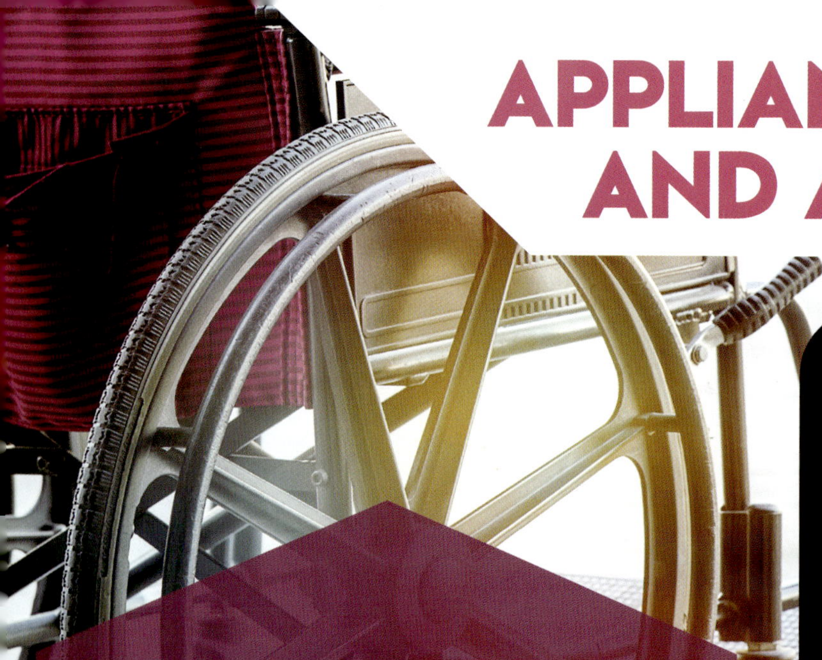

APPLIANCES AND AIDS

Domestic appliance design has strong growth as the number and range of time-saving electrical goods, particularly those for the kitchen, keep increasing. Another expanding field is the design, manufacture and service of aids and equipment that can increase the independence of people with health and mobility problems or disabilities.

INDUSTRIAL DESIGNER

JOB DESCRIPTION

Industrial designers develop and prepare products for manufacture and often specialise in an area such as toys, car components, furniture or medical equipment. They explore the options and solutions for a product, taking into account manufacturing processes, marketing and the budget. They work on developing products that are functional, easy to use and that look appealing. Industrial designers focus on the overall structure of a product. Other members of the design team then focus on specific elements such as the electronic or mechanical parts.

RANGE OF WORK:

- prepare sketches
- use drafting software
- build and test models and prototypes
- select components and materials
- resolve assembly and manufacturing issues

EDUCATION AND TRAINING

There are diploma courses in product design and a number of degrees in industrial design. Most people complete a degree in design, engineering or industrial design at university. There can be strong competition for jobs in this field.

ELECTRONIC SERVICE TECHNICIAN

JOB DESCRIPTION

Electronic service technicians repair broken electronic machines and household appliances.

RANGE OF WORK:

- inspect and test components and equipment
- detect and diagnose faults
- adjust, align and repair electronic equipment
- complete maintenance reports

EDUCATION AND TRAINING

To become an electronic services technician requires the completion of an apprenticeship or traineeship. Electronic service technicians need excellent hand-eye coordination, and to enjoy technical activities.

REHABILITATION ENGINEER

JOB DESCRIPTION

A rehabilitation engineer designs systems and devices that improve the quality of life for people with disabilities and make it easier for them to do day-to-day things. It is a specialist field within biomedical engineering. Rehabilitation engineers might work at a rehabilitation centre, hospital, aids and equipment supplier or a biomedical engineering firm.

RANGE OF WORK:

- design equipment such as wheelchairs, hoists and beds
- test the safety, efficiency and effectiveness of equipment
- ensure the equipment meets Australian standards
- analyse and design orthotic and prosthetic devices, such as artificial limbs

EDUCATION AND TRAINING

People become rehabilitation engineers by completing a degree in mechanical engineering, mechatronic engineering or mechanical/ biomedical engineering.

MY STORY

I was 16 when I was fitted with my first prosthetic leg. At the time I thought that there must be more that could be done for amputees - better materials that could be used in the limbs and better ways to understand what a person needed. I went on to study a degree in prosthetics and orthotics. My work involves making and fitting prostheses and orthoses for amputees and people with disabilities.

If I am making an artificial leg, I first take measurements of the good leg so that the artificial leg will mimic this leg. With older people you have to assess whether they will have the strength to put a limb on, be able to get up on it and walk on it and have the eyesight and balance to cope with it. When making the artificial limb, every step is done by hand. We only use machines to grind and sand the edges of the limb. After fitting the limb, you watch a person walk to check that the limb is level, that they are walking straight and have a good stride and support.

Although the field is very small, it is growing. It's exciting as we are using more space-age materials, hydraulics and computers. It's also a job that provides a lot of job satisfaction.

A few words of advice:
It is a very hands-on job, as a computer won't do the work for you. You need good hand-eye coordination, the ability to carry out mathematical calculations and a good understanding of physics and biomechanics.

'You need a good understanding of physics'

GEORGIOS KALAREMAS
PROSTHETIST AND ORTHOTIST

FASHION AND FURNITURE

The people who sell clothes, accessories, furniture and homewares are only one segment of those employed in the fashion and furniture industries. There are people who design and make fabric, source and buy fabric for manufacturers and designers, design clothing and furniture items and are involved in the making or manufacturing of these items.

• TEXTILE DESIGNER

JOB DESCRIPTION

Fabric is used to make a variety of items around the home including clothes, couches, curtains, cushions, bed linen, car seats and luggage. It is the role of the textile designer to design and develop fabric for these products. Textile designers consider how a fabric looks and how it will perform under the conditions it will most likely endure. Designing fabric requires decisions about colours, patterns, textures, thickness and weight.

RANGE OF WORK:

- develop the fabric concept into artwork
- develop colour specifications
- prepare instructions for the production of fabrics
- monitor trends and predict future trends.

EDUCATION AND TRAINING

There are several diploma and degree courses at TAFEs and universities in design, textiles and fashion that prepare people for a career in textile design.

• FURNITURE MAKER

JOB DESCRIPTION

Furniture makers, also known as artistic carpenters, make furniture from solid timber, flat-panel or timber-based products. Furniture makers can be employed by furniture manufacturers, restoration companies or cabinetmakers. They might be self-employed.

RANGE OF WORK:

- read and interpret plans
- select and prepare timber or board
- mark and cut shapes
- reinforce joints
- fit hinges, locks, catches and shelves

EDUCATION AND TRAINING

Furniture makers usually complete an apprenticeship.

• JEWELLER

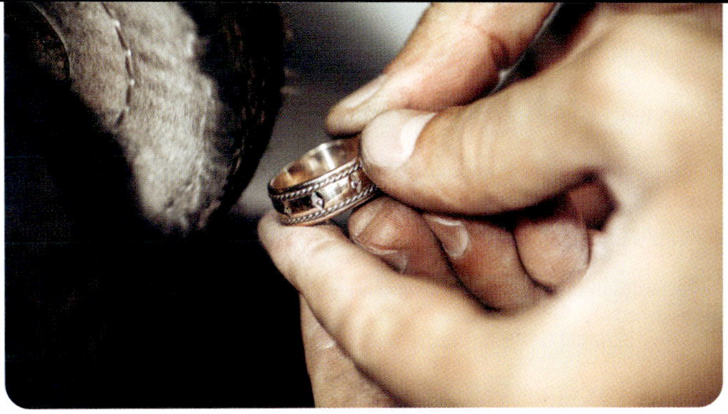

JOB DESCRIPTION

Jewellers design and make items such as rings, brooches, bracelets, necklaces, watches and earrings. They might specialise in a particular type of jewellery, such as diamond rings, or in a particular technique such as engraving or enamelling. Precious metals, stones, woods, plastics and leather are the materials that jewellers most commonly work with.

RANGE OF WORK:

- shape materials by cutting, heating, filing, hammering or bending
- use power tools to shape and finish items
- remodel and repair old jewellery
- set stones

EDUCATION AND TRAINING

Jewellers usually complete an apprenticeship that combines learning the craft on-the-job with studying for a certificate at a TAFE college.

MY STORY

When I was young I always loved to wear special clothes. It was my dream to be a designer. I studied fashion for three years at TAFE. I did find it a hard course, but I loved it. When I finished I found it difficult to find a job. I grew up in Afghanistan and India and only came to Australia six years ago, so I didn't know many people in the industry.

I worked with a designer doing pattern-making and grading, which is where you work out the sizes and cut the fabric. Then lots of people started asking me to do things for them, which was great.

I also kept doing my own sketches because I had so many of my own ideas and I really wanted to have my own label. Now I'm working on my own label, called Neelofar. I do cocktail and evening wear.

It's a lot of fun. The best part is the fashion parades and getting the feedback. I never get tired of my work - it's like meditation to me. When I create something and it comes up nicely it makes me incredibly happy.

A few words of advice:
Work with different designers so that you get experience doing lots of things. It's easier if you have worked for someone else for a few years before starting your own business. In fashion you just have to go for it. You can't wait for someone to come to you to offer you a job.

'When I create something, it makes me incredibly happy'

NEELOFAR AZIMI
FASHION DESIGNER

DESIGN AND PRODUCTION

The entertainment industry employs a range of people with artistic, creative and technical skills. Jobs in this area range from the semi-skilled to the highly skilled and specialised.

• SET/STAGE DESIGNER

JOB DESCRIPTION

Set and stage designers are involved in the creation of television programs, films and stage productions. Working closely with the director, producers and tradespeople, they research, design and supervise the construction of sets, scenery, props, costumes and visual aids.

RANGE OF WORK:

- produce sketches and scale models
- design sets and props that are within budget and meet technical requirements
- supervise a construction team
- advise on lighting and sound

EDUCATION AND TRAINING

Many courses are available at the degree and diploma level that prepare people for a career in set and stage design. However, gaining hands-on experience is also important.

• MULTIMEDIA DEVELOPER

JOB DESCRIPTION

Multimedia developers are involved in the design and development of a range of communication and entertainment materials. This includes animated videos, electronic training and educational materials, web pages and screen savers. Multimedia uses a combination of text, images, sound, video and animation.

RANGE OF WORK:

- assess and select software and equipment
- prepare diagrams and storyboards to outline a concept
- prepare 2D and 3D animations and images

Multimedia developers often specialise in specific areas such as computer animation, digital video, sound editing or game development.

EDUCATION AND TRAINING

Multimedia developers usually have qualifications in multimedia, graphic design or an area of IT. A large number of courses in multimedia are available at certificate, diploma and degree levels.

PRINTER

JOB DESCRIPTION

Printers use sophisticated printing machines to manage the printing of products such as magazines, labels, boxes, wrappers and newspapers. Printing machines are computer controlled and can be worth anything from $50,000 to $5 million.

RANGE OF WORK:

- output graphic images onto plate or press
- prepare machines
- prepare ink and additives
- apply quality checks
- undertake production scheduling
- prepare cost estimates

EDUCATION AND TRAINING

Education for printers involves on-the-job training as well as undertaking a certificate level course.

SCREEN PRINTER

JOB DESCRIPTION

Screen printers design and apply words and graphics to various materials, such as clothes, cardboard, stickers and posters. It is a trade that suits creative people who enjoy working with a variety of surfaces and colours.

RANGE OF WORK:

- prepare stencils for printing
- choose, mix and match coloured inks
- load materials into printing machines
- dry print items using hot air or ultraviolet light
- clean and maintain machines

EDUCATION AND TRAINING

Education for screen printers involves on-the-job training as well as undertaking a certificate level course.

'If you're interested in animation, start now'

MY STORY

A big part of my role as producer involves making sure that our projects get produced on time and to budget. I think of new ways to market our products and get them out there to the rest of the world. My background is in event management and business management.

A few words of advice:
As well as the desire and passion to be an animator, you need strong communication skills and a level of artistic ability. If you're interested in animation, start now. Even if it is just drawing your own cartoons at home.

RACHAEL PERRY
ANIMATION PRODUCER

PARKS AND GARDENS

People who design and construct public areas need to understand the reasons why people visit or use the area. They need to consider the amount of foot traffic that paths, lawns and tracks will have to withstand. A park's design needs to suit as many people as possible, be able to withstand long, continued use and be environmentally sustainable.

• PLAYGROUND DESIGNER

JOB DESCRIPTION

Playground designers design playgrounds that are imaginative, colourful, safe, and spark the imagination and interest of children. Some playground designers also design skate parks and BMX tracks. A playground designer is usually contracted to design and sometimes manage the construction of a playground.

RANGE OF WORK:

- discuss ideas and budget with a client
- analyse the needs of children who will be using the playground
- ensure the equipment can be used by children with disabilities
- produce concepts and plans that include equipment, shade, fencing and soft surfaces

EDUCATION AND TRAINING

Playground design is a small specialist field. It is common for people working is this area to hold qualifications in landscape architecture, design, industrial design or engineering.

• LANDSCAPE ARCHITECT

JOB DESCRIPTION

Landscape architects can design home gardens, but usually plan and design large, open outdoor areas. This includes shopping centres, holiday resorts, airports, parks and playgrounds.

RANGE OF WORK:

- discuss ideas, concepts, needs and budgets with clients, consulting engineers, architects and other professionals regarding soil structure, conservation issues and drainage
- prepare sketches, plans and detailed drawings showing garden beds, paths, water features, seats, bike paths and buildings

EDUCATION AND TRAINING

To become a landscape architect, you must complete a landscape architecture degree, gain work experience.

HORTICULTURALIST

JOB DESCRIPTION

Horticulturalists must have extensive knowledge of plants and how they are grown. They need to understand flowers, trees, shrubs and vegetables and should be able to select and match these plants to the environments in which they can thrive. Their roles can be diverse according to the area they work in or care for. For example, the work of a horticulturalist could include researching the development of fruit and vegetable crops or maintaining a council park. This is very different from the work of a horticulturalist who cares for plants in a retail nursery, who might give advice and sell plants to customers.

RANGE OF WORK:

- maintain soil and apply treatments and fertilisers to promote strong plant growth
- select locations for different types of plants
- plan, design and prepare garden beds with appropriate light, moisture and nutrients
- construct horticultural features including rock gardens, paths and ponds
- instal and operate sprinkler and irrigation systems
- prune trees and hedges
- control pests and ensure plants have adequate water

EDUCATION AND TRAINING

Horticulturalists undertake an apprenticeship where they combine study at a TAFE or a registered training authority with hands-on practical experience. There are also diplomas and advanced diplomas in horticulture.

MY STORY

When I left school, I knew I wanted to work with and around plants. I really enjoyed the visual impact that plants can have but I also like the way they can affect people's lives and change the way that they feel day-to-day.

I enjoy horticulture because it has many different facets. I started work in ornamental horticulture and have worked in a few different areas to get a broad range of experience. I have looked after period-style Victorian gardens, commercial landscapes and ornamental roof gardens. Now, I create community gardens in disadvantaged areas. I really like the variety of work I do, but also how I get to engage with people to create green urban places.

Currently, I'm working to support diverse communities to grow their own food. I get to experience many different foods and many different cultures, all while sharing a love of plants. It's great how plants can create opportunities for people to connect, working side-by-side and sharing their stories as social therapy. Through plants, we are able to work together to change the environment and the lives of those we love, our community elders and our young people. Working with plants can open the door to new interests or to volunteer work in the field of horticulture.

A few words of advice:
Make sure you get some hands-on experience in horticulture. Whether you want to be a landscape designer or work in garden maintenance, you'll need to know what a garden needs all year round. In horticulture, you never stop learning so keep trying new things and growing different plants.

'try new things and grow different plants'

PHIL PETTITT
COMMUNITY GREENING MANAGER

EXCITING TIMES

The world is changing faster than ever and designers play an important role in shaping that future. They think about how the future looks and what people need and want.

ARTIFICIAL INTELLIGENCE

Artificial intelligence is a huge area that is advancing rapidly and designers are creating a range of products to meet growing consumer demand.

MULTI-SENSORIAL DESIGN

Multi-sensorial design is gaining momentum in many different areas. This type of design involves engaging all five senses: sight, hearing, touch, taste and smell.

SOCIAL DESIGN

Social design is a growing field that uses ideas which create a better future for society, rather than just better products.

GET FUTURE READY

If you think you might be interested in a career in design or construction, there are a few things that you can do right now that might be useful later. Why not research your education pathways to see what options are available to you? Maybe you could plan the qualification route that you might like to follow, or investigate the practical steps you could take to gain experience in the types of work that interest you.

THE FUTURE

PRACTICAL EXPERIENCE

- find work experience in a relevant area
- offer your services as a garden hand or labourer
- start a vegetable garden at home or garden club at school
- practice your drawing skills, both technical and artistic and start creating a portfolio
- talk to people who work in similar jobs
- read as much as you can about the job
- check what qualifications are needed
- research the job on the Internet

DO YOU NEED QUALIFICATIONS?

There are many different levels of qualifications and training opportunities for jobs in design and construction. Some jobs can be entered into straight from secondary school, but most require TAFE certificates, diplomas and often a university degree. Engineers in most fields have postgraduate qualifications and the field of architecture can be very competitive. The more qualifications you have, the more likely you are to get a job in your chosen field. At school, you can keep your options open by doing a variety of hands-on subjects and keeping up with your maths skills.

GLOSSARY

amenities public facilities, such as toilets and showers

amputees people who have had a limb, such as an arm or leg, removed

autopilot navigational device that automatically keeps planes, ships and spacecraft on course

bevelling shaping an edge

corrosion the wearing away or rusting of materials

detonators small explosive devices used to make another substance or object explode

doggers construction workers who apply slings to loads being moved by cranes and who direct crane drivers

elevations heights above ground level of structures

enamelling applying a glassy glaze substance to a surface to protect against rust or corrosion

excavate dig large holes

fixtures fixed or attached items such as light fittings, door handles and sinks

foundations concrete slabs or stumps that support buildings

foundries factories producing metal castings

hydraulics using water under pressure to make something else move

infrastructure structures that allow other activities to happen, such as schools, hospitals and roads

irrigation adding water to crops, often by diverting the flow of rivers to farms

orthotic devices that help support and realign the body

pre-apprenticeship TAFE certificate course that can lead to an apprenticeship with an employer

prosthetic artificial extension of the body

prototype original design model, which is copied and replicated

riveting joining two materials together using bolts known as rivets

scaffolders people who assemble and take down scaffolding which provides a safe platform for workers to stand on while working at heights

smelters industrial plants where ore is melted to extract the metal

soldering using melted metals to join pieces of metal

TAFE Technical And Further Education

tenders detailed documents that outline how a project will be completed

INDEX